HOUSE OF MIRRORS

HOUSE OF MIRRORS

poems by
Joseph Hutchison

JAMES ANDREWS & CO., INC.
Publishing
Golden, Colorado

Cover Art: ''House of Mirrors'' by Patty Miller, reproduced courtesy of the artist
Book Design: Marilyn Auer, *The Bloomsbury Review*, Denver, Colorado
Composition: 11 point Bembo, Argent Typographics, Inc., Boulder, Colorado
Printed and Bound: McNaughton & Gunn, Inc., Lithographers, Saline, Michigan

Copyright © 1992 by Joseph Hutchison
Library of Congress Card Number: 91-71398
ISBN 0-9614643-3-X

ACKNOWLEDGMENTS

Grateful acknowledgment is made to the editors of the following publications in which many of these poems first appeared, often in different versions: *The Agni Review, American Poetry Review, Aspen Anthology, Brix Magazine, The Chariton Review, The Chowder Review, Colorado Review, Concerning Poetry, The Denver Quarterly, Grasshopper, The Hague Review, The Hudson Review, Images, The Little Review, Massachusetts Review (Poetry on the Buses), Mississippi Review, The Nation, New Mexico Humanities Review, Northeast, The Ohio Review, Portland Review, Prism International, Puerto Del Sol, Rapport, Rocky Mountain Review, South Dakota Review, West Branch, The Windflower Home Almanac of Poetry, Writers Forum,* and *Yes Magazine.*

"Walking Off a Night of Drinking in Early Spring" appears in *Luna: Myth and Mystery* by Kathleen Cain (Johnson Books, 1991). "Grace" and "Crossing the River" appear in *The Decade Dance* (Sandhills Press, 1991). "Catacombs" appears in the anthology *Movieworks* (Little Theatre Press, 1990). "Thunderhead" and "Walking Off a Night of Drinking in Early Spring" appear in *Crossing the River: Poets of the Western United States* (Permanent Press, 1987). "St. Patrick's Day Blues" and "Wandering Music" appear in *City Kite on a Wire: An Anthology of Denver Poets* (Mesilla Press, 1986). "Internal Combustion" and "From the Family Album" appear in *Wingbone: Poetry From Colorado* (Sudden Jungle Press, 1986). "House of Mirrors," under the title "This Year," appears in the anthology *American Classic* (SCOP Publications, 1985), in *The Ohio Review's Ten-Year Retrospective Issue* (June, 1983), and in *The Anthology of Magazine Verse* (Monitor Book Company, 1981).

Certain of these poems have also appeared in the following chapbooks: *Wandering Music* (Juniper Press, 1990), *Thirst* (Juniper Press, 1984), in *Shadow-Light* (a limited edition of 10 copies handmade by artist Judy Anderson for the 1982 Colorado Governor's Awards), and in *Weathers, Vistas, Houses, Dust* (Juniper Press, 1980).

Italicized portions of "Elegy for Michael, a Friend, Killed in His Car" are reworked borrowings from "The Wanderer," translated by Michael Alexander and included in his Penguin Classics anthology, *The Earliest English Poems.*

Acknowledgment is also made to the following for permission to reprint copyrighted material:
Beacon Press: Quotation from *The Poetics of Space,* Gaston Bachelard, translated by Maria Jolas.
The Ecco Press: Excerpt from "To a Young Poet Who Fled," copyright © 1955, 1960, 1961, 1962, 1963, 1964, 1965, 1966, 1967, 1968, 1969, 1970, 1973, 1981 by John Logan. From *Only the Dreamer Can Change the Dream,* first published by The Ecco Press in 1981. Reprinted by permission.
The University of New Mexico Press: Quotation from *The Legend of Ogden Jenks* by Robert Emmitt.

Special thanks to Gary Schroeder for his close reading of this book in manuscript.

For my parents, Joe and Helen,
for Susannah and Brian,
and for Melody

CONTENTS

I
HOUSE OF MIRRORS

There was a murmur like water
draining through pipes, and he felt
he had awakened. Out the window,

a whole hillside covered
with men, women, and children
(mostly different shades
of brown) who were starving
in gray light. And that light
seemed the oddest part—

dissolving the scene
like a time-lapse film of mold
fuzzing an apple . . . or the way,
after late shows, Old Glory
decays into empty snow.

*

Thinned by the Sony, Enesco's
Rumanian Rhapsody woke him
truly. After a while he got up,

bathed and dressed. In the chilly
gray kitchen, he filled a bowl
from a cereal box that offered—for

fifty cents plus three proofs of purchase—
photographs of certain creatures soon
to die out. Part of a series:

"The Vanishing Breeds."

THE GEESE

Across from the bus stop,
a pair of plump Canada
geese are flatfooting down
the clumpy knoll. Their rumps
sway, their draggled heads
darting glances to every side.
Just fifty wild generations back
such looks must have outfoxed
foxes; but here, in this
tiny suburban park laid out
among fenced-in houserows,
such wariness seems comical—
Ralph Cramden and Oliver Hardy
sneaking home after a night
with the boys. . . .
                    How this
century of images has darkened
my spirit! Much as the park's
pond waters have darkened: tainted
by road salt, mercury, malathion;
exhausted by decorator faucets,
by hoses, sprinklers and gutters.
So much of ourselves in those
furtive creatures; so much
of our lives in the shallow,
clouded waters.

AT THE ARTS FUNDRAISER

for David Guerrero

Each of their walls is adorned
with the trash of privilege. Here,
gashes of scarlet, dark blues,
and earthtones in the scalloped
force field of a gilt frame; there,
wool that's been dyed and resurrected
as kachinas, turquoise and russet,
splayed upon a warm black sky.
"We collect," the host tells us,
swerving into talk of bond markets
and interest rates.
          I need a drink,
and quit his company; but return
later with a Southern Comfort
glowing in my fist, and examine
the walls. Glossies of our hostess
hugging Pavarotti (at bottom, a scrawl
reading: "Ciao! Luciano—"); another
on the slopes with Billy Kidd;
another on the golf course at Vail,
waving to us all from the arms
of ex-president Ford.
          Suddenly
I hear the ice cracking in my glass,
and think: *They collect.* And I see
the good cause that brought me here
obliges me to face such walls, wailing
in silence like a Jew at the Kremlin,
gnawing the bone of my contention,
swallowing words like these.

GRANDMA

Eating earned us her grace: almonds
like chunks of moon, red candy apples,
potato chips, Coke. We'd joke about her
while nursing her creamy nutmeg malts.
She gave us dollars rolled up like buds,
and we spent them on gumballs and trinkets.

Now, when we hug her, we recall our clever
kibitzing: how she heard, but always let
the lamplight flash her bifocals blank;
how she rocked, crocheting the coarse
yarn of her starved youth into slippers,
whose warmth we wore to rags on the street.

THIRST

A gricf springs up
at our feet
bitter black
cold water

as if from another life
where every joy fails

till our faith
in this earth gives
way like river ice
beneath a boot

and kneeling
down in our shadow
our animal shadow
we drink

there is no end
to this drinking

AFTER THE ATTACK

for my father

I

White-smocked and wired, pulse
a fainting brightness on the gray
screen, you lay strapped down
by tubes and heavy ropes of
fatigue. Breath a muffled stutter.
Your hand crawls blind on the sheet.
A bottle of healing fluid feeds
your forearm, its veins made blue
by thirst. My love, too, is a kind
of nectar, which enters you
through the needle of my grief.

II

For years you sat up nights,
sleepless, nursing your worries
and Lucky Strikes, sucking down
smoke like noxious milk. Each
drag darkly lit your face, eyes
wan as winter moons. In your groin
the clock's gossip coiled, tight
as spring steel. Then a word—
Oregon—opened your dreams, rich
with the promise of rivers and fields:
in your body, the lost sun blossomed.

III

My thought like a wild bee darts
around what staggers on the screen;
your heart's rosebud, my father, is
delicate, quivering in its thorns.
I want to enter that frail firecoal,
to feel its cracked-bell resonance.
I've kept a shut door between us,
never hearing your petal-gloved
mortal knock. Now the door is split,
unhinged: shoots of new light arrow in.
Sparks of dust blow through the shaken air.

IV

Awakened, you touch my hand lightly
as a mother's, then unwind into sleep
once more. Your eyes, in their thin
wrinkling jackets, roll as if you are
flying over the fields you wanted; dew
brushed from the young wheat gathers
on your brow. I feel dawn breathe
over the land, and the greenest stalks
bristle up suddenly ripe, a red-gold
morning storm: their roots (long tongues
of slow lightning) dig to taste dark water.

PNEUMONIA

Stars through the windshield glinted,
shrunken, delirious as the eyes
of sharks. I heard mother's
heart (my head
cradled in her elbow's
crook) chant *faster*, and father
tramped down the pedal
when his lane was clear. Later,

lungs drowning in my chest, I sucked
at oxygen fresh from a tank. Thin
voices leaked in, trembling
the tent's wrinkled,
transparent skin. My mother's
face was a pale smear on the air,
her jacket a haggard ghost. "Doctor,"

father said. (I remembered his brown
palms, coarser than emery cloth
on my back, circling slowly
to draw insomnia from my blood;
the fat scar barnacled on
his thumb would whisper
along my ribs: *A man becomes
all that he's lost.*) He rasped,
"Doctor . . . will he die?" I let

go: the hiss of piped air drowned
his answer. And when I came to,
they were gone. Bones of cold light
flickered above my bed; hot urine
eeled between my legs and froze;
fins, in my fever's depths, ripped
through swelling tides of sleep:

the blackness swallowed its stars.

HOMING

for my mother

I almost remember my first haven: deep
in your body, alive with music. It seemed
a tide was pounding some distant cliffs,
and I lay adrift in a ship made of listening,
my sleep one long whole note drawn out
from a cello's chest.
                        But I was rescued
into light, and its pain—lifted and laid
down in this body, far inland.
                        Twenty years
it took to rediscover your cadence—not
ocean, but human: your spirit not moonlight
glossing the furrowed water, but a needle
quivering in time's spiral groove; passages
now faint, now loud as the fearsome knock
Beethoven heard.
                        How it hurts! Knowing
what sustained me all those shadowy hours
must end. And yet, the more I listen, I find
your music growing more lovely, more clear,
as it homes on into its silent center.

THE REFUGE

The saw's whine leaps out of my neighbor's garage and gnaws my sleep. I feel my bones creak with desire, bones that once swayed like green branches in a steaming forest, before the flood wrapped them in silt and blood. They want to be split, squared, smoothed; it is a longing for nails, to be shingles and beams. They dream of being rooted salt-white in the sun, erect in the winds off the mountains.

I curl up in the space between heartbeats, within these thick, fragile walls. *Pull down the shades*, my bones whisper. *Bolt the door. Be silence. Be darkness. Be dust.*

GHAZAL OF THE WAKEFUL NIGHT

The dying fire mutters and hugs its frail light;
those chilly chimney-gusts just won't let it sleep.

Dragged from the river, an unknown child. Yet how
heavily her absence rides in my shadow's black wagon!

Like desire, gravity measures our fear of vanishing;
as though earth, if we'd let it, would let us go.

Restless, the widow clears the pane with her sleeve.
But their child sleeps curled around his own breathing.

Cold splashed water hugs the campfire's coals, freeing
a tall ghost: star-haunter; bitter-breath; wanderer.

THUNDERHEAD

A tall cloud sleepwalks
out of mountains. Its weight
—the memory of
a drowned child—bows
down my head . . . as when
a plunging elevator
suddenly slows:
held breath; the heart-valve
struggle of the doors. Already

the storm's an abandoned
steeple, father-shaped, bell
a coyote's muzzle blurred
by a shower curtain. Underfoot,
my toes feel the grass
of a bathmat weave
and unweave the light
of my feelings, the oblique
shadow-light. Far off, I know

the child's kneeling again
by the flood stream. His milky
face on the swirls seems
weightless,
a cloud. As always, he
bends to touch it: how motherly
and dark my current's pull!
I gaze up at him
and smile. But when his arms
embrace me, the old panic
breaks their hold—

and the dream river
turns to a ditch
of red mud, down which the howls
that wake me vanish
like thunder.

MOUNTAIN FLOWER

for David

The way August heat makes horizons
tremble I
think of you

hummingbird whose wings
baffle and stir

there's a flower
standing by a dirt road inside me
columbine thistle or
what I can't say
for the dust of my passage whirls
around it and will
not settle

fly
through that wind you must
single out
the blossom I lost
in the narrow glance backward
of my mirror

part the petals brother
open it and drink
it is

unreal otherwise

EQUINOX AT THE RAINBOW HILL RANCH

for Bill and Betty

Matted in early light, the grass
uncurls around the ankles of the cows:
damp smoke. The barn's still dark,

walls wet; the sodden beams creak
in rootless sleep; and sharpened
by the cold, a fragrance of cut hay

broods over the clank of an iron bell.
Only those fruit-laden trees, bent
low, seem buoyant. I can almost hear

the round earth whispering its story
to the seeds . . . feel the season
holding its breath to listen.

GARLIC

Split-lip, shrunken
pucker like a mummy's,
your savor a breath held

under the earth; biter
of tongues, sullen
flame that chars

every throat, I
taste the dry ground
you root in, taste

the eye you lift up
to the sun. You're harsh
as sea-salt baked

onto oars
that once hauled ships
to Carthage. Oh kiss

of thirsty dust,
most ancient familiar
of the dead, you've

seasoned my voice
with a smoky
residue of time.

GHAZAL OF REVERIES

Where the ocean begins, so the journey.
Listening sails far into the roaring shell.

Skimming deep water, a lighthouse beam.
Who nailed this wing to my forehead?

The actor, hunting out survivors, lets his
searchlight drift over faces in the audience.

My pillow harbors a pulse, a surflike sound.
Dreaming feathers riffle in a windy sky.

From the mime's muscular wrists, dead
birds dangle. Flutter. Suddenly fly up!

FACING THE SEA

Here again

at the cliff's edge I find myself
one foot held out

if there are rocks below
I can't see them
only the foam's white scrawl
like words I can't make
fit the music

would it be
so much I wonder one step

the tide's hard kiss

but silence
silence is another matter

if I knew that what I hear is
the clear speech of an ocean slurred
by the senses
not merely my troubled blood
in its circular sleep

if only I knew
one step
would let me absolutely hear it

I might enter
the vastness of its voice

and know what names it repeats
what names I've forgotten
all of my life

maybe only my own

but clearly

FROM A TOUR BOAT ON CRATER LAKE

for Reg Saner

Here, Mount Mazama crashed
into itself, its being
a storm that burned its way out.
Then centuries of rain. So that now

the pit's wider than vision admits:
the roar of our motor strikes
the far cliffs softly
as some mosquito's whisper.
Beneath us, the water's
too pure for this world, richer
than bruise or bliss. And yet
we have seen it before: how light,
returning from any abyss, is
always this color: a violet so deep

that the heart mutters
bottomless, hangs
in the ribcage suddenly heavy,
ripe with the blood's buried thunder.

ROBERT EMMITT

<blockquote>
"He got hisself all to hisself."
                    —*The Legend of Ogden Jenks*
</blockquote>

They'd shut the blinds against the bright
April day, alive with unseasonable snow,
but the air in your room still glittered,
each second's crystal pattern unrepeatable—
a storm your face was the calm center of.
                              Bob,
I gossiped and smiled, though your dry mouth
gaped under stroke-emptied eyes; I knew
it was reflex, yet felt somehow you'd fallen
down a well and hung there treading water,
too wise to lavish breath on speech.
Truth is, of course, you couldn't speak,
or even signal you'd like to speak.
                         Truth is
I invented the well just now—and it stands
for my own trapped feeling, not yours.
I hated your being so shattered, so damned
reducible! And so drew a meaning image
from your stare, as if I'd read it there.
What *did* you want? Working your tongue
as if tasting the memory of gruel, or
the first time a burst vessel felled you
face down in the dirt. I remember touching
your shaved head, warm as lichened stone,
your cheeks baby-bottom smooth.
                          Truth
is, what I wished for you then was death,
easeful death. But you waited—lingered
into June, and died on my birthday. I told
the news at my party, and Joe said, "He hoped
we'd all talk about him." And we did. We do.
Old friend, both of our wishes came true.

Toward midnight I conjure the intersection:
sparkle of glass in gutters, a fanbelt
snapped, the hosed–off asphalt slick
and rainbowed with oil. Under my shirt,
a groundswell of dark breath . . . *sorrow
and sleep banded together.*
                    And his face
rises, clear as the prose mad Ireland
hurt him into, or the full moon
that followed us home from Nebraska.
The potholed roads rolled thunder
through our bones, shouldered us
toward ditches flooded with shadows. . . .
"One summer I worked on a highway," he said.
"Listen, Joe. It was hard labor. But come
day's end, I could measure my effort:
so many yards of fresh pavement.
Not like this writing business." *Alone
am I driven, each day before daybreak,
to give my cares utterance.* I dream him
bent over his writing table, mourning
its fabulous litter. "You enter a world
and make it real," he said. I almost hear,
on his closed boat's bow, the measured
slap and kiss of the exiling sea,
bearing him toward shores of origins
and silence. . . .
                  But my sullen heart's
own noise drowns it out. *Friends
are lent us, kin lent. All the earth
shall stand empty.* Again, the jolt
and weave of our wandering car
on those roads, the bruised moon
low over haunted fields. I believed
he slept in the dashboard glow, slumped
against his door; but the evening's
dishevelled sparkle moved him. "Jaysus,"
said he, "it's a dark world." Now
darker still, and each breath labored,
as the clock's two spectral hands touch,
shine . . . slowly let each other grow dim.

AFTER THE BATH

She towels her freshly
washed thighs
where my blind fingers pried
like roots: desire
lifted

out of me
a tall tree of breath;

for a moment, her name
slept in its shadow.
But now, eyes

holding some inward image,
she bends forward
(smiling
to herself)
and breathes in

the soap's clean scent.
Absently swaying,

she buffs her breasts till
the soft nipples wake—
sunrise pink.

PRIVACY

Naked, you lie
like a white villa by the sea,
shutters thrown open.
I drift through your rooms,
sunlit, nameless . . .
like dust.

DRIVING HOME

Crossing Idaho the road was potholed ice.
Miles rumbled through our bodies, what vigor
the motel beds had left us shaken loose.
The sky whitened into another sleep.
Our eyes snagged spidery telephone lines
that pulled them toward the buildings
scattered in snow like dice—dark bones
some sucker rolled, loaded to lose.

Over one 50-mile stretch thawed slick
as sleight-of-hand by the owl-gazing sun,
our wheels gambled on the slush. But passing
a Cadillac tight with faces, we fishtailed
blind, swerving like a hooked steelhead,
and tobagganed into the median ditch. Jill
gunned us back up to the road and across
to a stop on the shoulder. Then the Caddy
eased by, dwindling eastward, trivial.

No sounds but Idaho wind; snow grains
teething on metal; the magical, throaty
steadiness of the motor. We breathed.
Our voices quivered like bad connections,
splintering words. Then quiet, we heard
our hearts spinning their blood—gossamer
frail—and held each other till bone
kissed bone through the skin.

VIEWPOINT ON INDEPENDENCE PASS

Cold wind

flooding the tundra turns
our skin to blown
lake water
the roots of our vanished
fur gripping down

but the bare peaks stare
us back through the blood's
animal noise
back
into bone time silence
of boulders sunk
up to the eyebrows
in ooze

back to the first dream

dim sense
that the possible surrounds us
clear as glacial water
which our least
attempt to ascend through
would cloud

but clear
as if we might ascend

knowing the shadows fish
kiss us with
will one day turn
into birds

knowing
that finding us drowned
today in our bodies this wind
will have so
surrounded
and awakened us

that we suddenly feel
kissed by shadows of birds
sailing high
in the gusty light

THE CALENDAR CANDLE: BURNING THE FIRST MONTH

for Jon and Terre

A blue snow at the flame's center, like the dust our body gathers in its unused rooms . . . dust that wanders blindly when any door in the house swings open. All around the stiff, twisted wick the little storm billows, confused . . . every moment of a man's life flying toward him . . . a swarm of returning leaves in which the naked tree shivers, struggling to hold its ground. . . .

But often, among those tangled branches, birds appear. They try the blizzard with bright red wings, uncertain . . . then simply let go. Diving up into high, rippling clarity, they float—longer than they'd hoped—before their glowing bodies turn black. . . .

GHAZAL OF THE UNBORN CHILD

for Pat and Lois

Between peaks and plains long abandoned by sea,
between two lovers, the thrash of white surf.

The sun remembers its life as a fish:
a pulse in the silence, electric. A word.

Like dreams, our heartland flies from shadow
to shadow, swiftly, on wings of dark water.

The knot of fire defines its round night;
lamp of flesh, phosphorescent desire.

We too were sunken and nameless, obscure;
then the moon untangled tides in our chests.

Twilight is deepening; a child must be growing.
The crimson star dances in the blackbird's throat.

ONE EVENING EARLY IN THE NEW YEAR

I

Our bodies' breath
clouds the cold windows.
Naked hips kissing, we slip

into our separate sleep.

II

I wake about eleven.

Secretly, over the panes,
drops have woven milk-white
threads of the full moon.

I've slept in five houses, but wakened
in one body over and over. My eyes
stung by headlights, sore-boned
at the struggling wheel, I've steered
our goods through each bad weather.
Now our blood's jazzed again
on thin air; the money's ample,
the Rockies huge. We feel
on our way somewhere.

And yet, I ache at how dreams
can swerve to a cliff-edge, wheels
holding barely. . . . I think
how prodigal longings are (sparks
echoed in a house of mirrors), how far
from home our destinations: Han-shan
high on Cold Mountain; Lowell
struck down in his cab.

1977

FALLING SILENT

Sunlight warms the lately wetted earth,
leavens it into an ashy dust the breeze
seems just about to lift. Across the yard,
a clumsy bee stumbles among lilac petals,
golden powder on his paintbrush feet.

I watch and doze, head solid on a root's
bent knee. Big limbs sway high in my dream,
leaf-shadows skittering over my eyelids: dark
and light; crimson and pink; flocks homing
into my skull. What can I rightly call them?

I glance down into confusions of grass. Oh,
let me lie here awhile and sleep. I will slip
free of words and their categorical heaven.
My arms snake around the roots of silence.
Ah mother! These fatal ambiguities of sense!

II
WANDERING MUSIC

I kiss your belly with
my right ear, hold
my breath. Underneath, each
heartfelt rush is weak as wind
in thick summer grass.

Susannah? Daniel?
No one, yet.

Yet a life—reach over
grasp—is climbing
the strong vine of its will
into the cradle-rocking boughs
of our human love.

Even the happiest of us
sometimes fears it's unreal:
after months or years, a flat
taste wakens in the mouth,
your eyes gone gray inside—
the way dying seems to insist
that life wasn't worth it,
when in fact it's all
time and luck making war,
or making love, who can tell.

A TRANSFORMATION

My hand was not my hand,
her wrist not the warm neck
of a white hen. My heart
hammered my eyes until she
hung before me: furious

holocaust of feathers
on a bare wall. But my hand
was not my hand! Her voice not
the beak that ripped the air
from groin to throat. No—

we became a different
species, then; not the man
and woman we are tonight:
bellies slapping in the darkness,
fingers digging, whispering of love.

RECURRING DREAM

Moonlight deep
in midnight grass:
standing pools.

I step in.
The stairway's long.
I climb down,

floating.
And a gentle voice
surges through the roots

of my inner ear: *Dear
brightness, archaic water,
spring all lovers ache*

to drink from. . . .
Far off,
an immense glass

standing on my bedtable
shines in the dark,
a moth

on the rim.
No—
not a moth:

my severed lips.

Stones on the corners of the picnic blanket, holding things down. That's their way, held down as they are by their own gravity. Not so the man and the woman who sip wine on the blanket, nibbling at bread, pâté and cheese so lightly, lightly. They look each other deep in the eyes. Now and then, they laugh without reason. If not for their bodies, they would drift off into the clear summer sky. Year after year we watch them grow lighter, until we feel afraid they'll desert us completely. For that reason, in the end, we'll hide them deep and lay stones upon them. In love's name, holding things down.

A few thousand yards west,
interstate; the city
a few miles east. And I've
sweated out weeks at a desk,
machine and human noise
making me sick
of listening. But here

the hills carry quietness toward evening,
the way a nurse bears a bowl of water
to bathe the fevered body. Like slanting
sunlight in which small things cast
long shadows, this silence
magnifies:

crickets spinning
dusk on their creaky spindles,
clack of locusts, the meadowlark
jazz. . . . And each breath
healing air to air,
pulse to music, in the deep
and hidden valleys of the chest.

AFTER A GLIB ESSAY ON JAMES WRIGHT

It's a kind of blindness, this
taking a man's anguish for an aspect
of style; the way his words snap

like maple limbs under the wet weight
of snow, the tender heartwood taken
for hard-core belief. Better

find the longing that pearls out
sticky with April sun; better
press it with the fingertips and wave

them under the nose: this sap is
glittery, sharply sweet. One
must hurt long to utter such words,

must live to make the rich light
climb within, drawing out of winter
the durable bud, the leaf, the blossom.

THE OPEN BOOK

42   The window's a page of starlight
        scrawled with branches; a face

        mooning there, its ghost breath
        blurring the script. I douse

        the lamp, and the face goes out
        over the city like glittering wind.

        Now my body is dark in the dark,
        illiterate; the unwritten book

        of my soul stands open: room
        in which all sleepwalkers wake.

THE MAP

for William Stafford

Again tonight your words
have come, simple as deer.
And now your moon, snowball
flung by a boy on the last
day of his childhood, melts
among boughs under my eyelids,
filling those animal prints
with cold light. I follow
that map, making my way deep
into the wilderness. There
I discover a house built
of shadow, a blood-red door,
a window where an old woman
parts her wizened lips . . . my name
blooming briefly on the glass.

THE NEXT ROOM

Speaking low to myself, I
hear in the next room my infant
daughter working her tongue,
wet and thoughtful. Is
she listening? Listening

to my worrying syllables,
this selfish music? Someday,
she may recall my cadence
and think it's a rush of blood—
her very own, as I imagine it

mine. But now I hear she's
sleeping at last. Working on,
I feel in my throat's well
some other's voice, as
stones in the rapids feel

thunder in their hearts—
wet and thoughtful. And if I
call it father (father
in the next room), I must
believe he hears and listens.

THE FACE

In the dream I lift up
my hand

the lamplight
bathes your long back
bare beneath a windowed moon

I came down the mountain
followed a thread of creek
through tangled bracken
naked under stars
that were no map to me
down I came with my lantern
and my bleeding feet
as always
in this dream
and lifted my hand

oh my life
turn

—or don't turn

this time I remember
your vacant face
its scars which I love

the reason you keep it hidden

INTERNAL COMBUSTION

I'm a responsible man, and so
they load me up. Seems they think
I'm a truck with a big engine,
thick tires, strong shock absorbers:
a little gas, some water, battery acid—
they think it keeps me happy.

But it happens I'm also a lamp
with a chimney of glass
and a bellyful of golden spice-oil.
It happens my tongue is a wick,
and when the longing
flames out from my furnace heart,
I speak, and those who listen
burn. Or I don't speak:
I swallow the fire,
and it sinks down writhing
in my scrotum like some demon.

It's that demon who lights my way.
The demon they name if they mention me.
The demon who drives me around in circles,
roaring like hell, eating my own sweet dust.

LIFTING MY DAUGHTER

As I leave for work she holds out her arms, and I
bend to lift her . . . always heavier than I remember,
because in my mind she is still that seedling bough
I used to cradle in one elbow. Her hug is honest,
fierce, forgiving. I think of Oregon's coastal pines,
wind-bent even on quiet days; they've grown in ways
the Pacific breeze has blown them all their lives.
And how will my daughter grow? Last night, I dreamed
of a mid-ocean gale, a howl among writhing waterspouts;
I don't know what it meant, or if it's still distant,
or already here. I know only how I hug my daughter,
my arms grown taut with the thought of that wind.

On tiptoe he reaches, hands it to me—
a polished dollop of moonlight, spiralled
as soft ice cream—and says, "Don't drop it."
His mother's voice, her caution. Or maybe
he's lived near me long enough to learn
something fearful about pretty things
that break, get broken. Oh, not by malice,
but a kind of fecklessness: how whatever
I take up can distract my grasp, any
subtle shape or mesmerizing sheen. Maybe
he sees I'm a man who lets lovely things go,
whose next lapse could silence the ocean
he has cradled in his own firm hands.

JONI MITCHELL

Water falls white on the white
washed stones, fingers
light on piano or the spine
of a lover.
Sobs and exultations,
the open mouths and eyes of astounded
houses, doves
dead in mid-air, a scatter
of leaves like torn astrologies.

With her voice full of swords and blossoms,
salt and blonde honey, voice
like the ruffle of air off the tip
of the heron's wing,
she sings the scrawl of blood
and the fiery scripture
of nerves
written under the skin.

We've slept like mountains, but now
drum and saxophone swim
in our bodies,
hook-jawed salmon that leap
the black keys, dying
for the drowned genital stars,
their fine bones singing like tuning forks.

And there are guitars
overflowing like drunken goblets,
shiny sea-turtles dragging
inland, heavy with eggs. There are
sparrows dreaming in the cradles of her wrists,
and roses, and ashes, and oceans
collapsing on empty beaches, sliding
back helpless and rising again.

SAINT PATRICK'S DAY BLUES

for Esther

Scratching the strings
of your guitar at the party,
shouting out blues, drunk
on my own eighty-proof
voice. Striking the sevenths,
mimicking Mike's ukelele.
Blowing it, fumbling,
losing the G. Then
finding it a fret away,
pure as the clear green marble
I found in the mud as a boy. The one
I picked up, held up into the June light.
Squinting. Eyeing the scars. Amazed
at the brightness of the scars.
I turned it in my grimy
ten-year-old hand, the marble
flickering, making a music
from the light. A music
as crazed as those
drunken blues I banged out,
scraping the strings
as my knuckles
bled . . . and me
not knowing it
till the song was over,
and I stared down
in wonder at my numb
and ragged fingers. Then
strummed again. The strings
gone sour with the punishment—
for which the only cure was
more: more whiskey, more
raw-handed blues. Embracing
the music. Hugging it. Holding on
tight to the scarred and shining body.

WALKING OFF A NIGHT OF DRINKING IN EARLY SPRING

for Joe Nigg

Through the budding elm branches, eyes
of traffic lights blink red to green;
the idled traffic surges forward in the dark—

and we stagger on down the alley, joyful,
voices loud and cloudy in the cold.
Where do these hours come from? Hours

when old wounds flare, and the night
opens, and pain boils up into conversation,
as if talk can heal. The sweating bottle

drifts hand to hand, mouth to mouth—
and stars blink through branching clouds,
the blood groping darkly in our heads;

but the moon's here, too: a bright clarity
over cars and streetlamps, over houses
and leaving trees: going with us.

The sky outside my window's gusty and ragged,
shape-shifting, queasy and bright. My head
crawls with blood and darkens, would peel
itself and bell-like hang, thinking *fuchsia*,

tenderly. There were fuchsias at Gold Beach
that week I read Rimbaud in a rented bed,
adrift between two foreign tongues—his French
and the argot my spirit used in poems (I believed

whatever it said had nothing to do with my life;
it didn't, therefore my anguish). I imagined
myself in Africa, or a pale version of it: secure
office work, weekends free for the *real* stuff—

that shit we writers cook up for ourselves to eat.
Yet my Africa's here, a landscape of cubicles—
doorless, fluorescent—where light-button phones
wink like idols. And my spirit has gone away

into the world: roofs and trees, then mountains,
then clouds into Utah and beyond. Last night
I was sick in the toilet, and later walked out
for a bath of sweet-cream moonlight, and thought

of the moon on the sea at Gold Beach, and the moon
in Rimbaud, the moon in my life. "You up there!"
I wanted to shout. "Yes! You know who I mean."
But I held back. And today: this wandering music.

VACATION

Thinking of going mad
isn't frightening. It's unreal—
like studying travel ads for Cozumel,
Jamaica, Tahiti . . . the beaches
blindingly white, the water
cerulean under plunging yachts
attended by bronzed women.
Madness is a rich man's sport,
and thinking of it makes you feel
the thinness of your wallet,
aching in your pocket
like a heart.

I keep dreaming of shells, or bits of them,
dizzy in the clear and shallow tidewater
that eased in and with a mild crash
washed my white feet, my ankles. Warm—
amazing how warm it was, the Florida water.
It had crawled all the miles from Nassau,
scouring mollusks out of their houses
gently, like souls from flesh . . . sun
brilliant upon its smooth body as it turned,
rolled and reached, half-sleeping, toward
my two pale legs. What a fine, aimless
feeling! Watching the trash of existence
dance all around me, in the flashing waves,
in memory: the beautiful wreckage. . . .

THE VOICE

An old toolshed in a shroud of lilacs. The wooden door loose,
held on by one rusted hinge and two long nails hammered flat.

Splintery June light. A somnolent dust on the rocks tumbled
out of the crumbling foundation. I think I mistook one
for a ball I'd lost last summer; but picking it up, felt
ants rain over my hands like cinders—and let it drop.

The cracked door shuddered in the windless silence.

And when the voice—angel's or demon's, I don't know—
issued from the shed, I could not move at first, my feet
sunk like fenceposts in the shadowed ground. *Come on,*
the voice crooned, as I stared into the slash-mouth
of blackness, holding my breath to keep my heart in.
God! How I bolted at last—scrambled across the sunlit
back yard and away, a darkness buzzing in my boyish head.

I drove that alley today, for no good reason. The shed's
gone, and the prodigal lilacs. Gone the deep voice now
that I need to hear it again, now that I know what to do.

I'd fall to my knees in the dirt, in the cool lilac-light.

Yes, I'd answer under my breath. And bend. And enter.

His hand has taken up the pen, but hesitates. The voices were
there a moment ago. Or one voice, a woman's. It woke him,
as if it came from just outside his half-open window. But now
there's only the whistly scraping of crickets in the night grass,
under the windless trees. Yet his hand feels alive with that lost
voice, and so he defers to the hand, which presently moves.
To the cricket noise it adds this other noise: the blind scratching
of a pen.

> These trees are still tonight. Look
> how the grass lays back. It needs cutting.
> Pour me another Frangelico,
> will you? There—
> I know, you think it's too sugary.
> You prefer that black ale,
> but only because it lets you fantasize
> about England. Go on, it's true. Anyplace
> but here, anyone but me. Oh,
> spare the denials!
> I didn't ask you here to argue.
> I'm *not* criticizing. Here,
> have a bite of this cake; I made it
> with you in mind. There's coal-colored
> bittersweet chocolate, with bits
> of hazelnut inside—the fruit
> Frangelico's made from. So you see,
> we do have something in common.
>
> My God, the trees are still! We're deep
> in the ditch of summer now. Stuck like stones.
> Summers are hardest. The bed feels bigger
> without the covers, emptier,
> though one keeps listening for a key
> in the lock, a footstep, a dresser drawer
> sighing open. The way the hangers ring
> in the closet when I take down a blouse—
> it goes right through me. . . .

Do you remember the summer we rode horses?
We were children, then. You were never
a child with *her*—but so what? I see now
that childhood was something you only
lived through. Like a marriage.
And I see the past still makes you grim.
I see lots of things now. Solitude
clarifies. Maybe that's why
those high country lakes were so
perfectly clear. Don't you remember?
How we rented horses and cantered
along the water, in the wind?
And the water was crystal, icy—
not blue the way children paint water,
but a dark silver, and the fish
were making bright rings everywhere,
and we barely spoke for all the looking.
Remember? We tied up the horses
to a pine tree knocked over by lightning
or wind. The roots were dry, twisted,
and the long body looked black
where it lay in the water. Farther out,
the clouds were hanging upside down
in the deeper water. We wasted
an hour or more skipping stones
across the clouds, then
raced each other into the meadow
like children. But we weren't children,
were we? Oh, it wasn't
what I used to think, that you saved me
from childhood, or that you ripped
childhood out of me. Somehow,
we'd agreed there was no future
in being children, and so
you hurt me into *this* world, you—
hurt me, yes. Don't give me
that fucking sigh! And please,
don't go. Pour me another. Please.

It's the damned trees. They make this
all so hard—as if they're watching.
We never were good at talking
in a crowd, were we? Oh,
we'd *chat.* And you were always
an entertainer. But talk
the way I mean it,
no. And then
we must have forgotten how
between ourselves. I remember
so little toward the end
but silence. . . .

Why don't the damned trees move?

August is cruelest, not April.
One can't even get drunk.

And so I long to be small again!
A small girl. Back when I had this
painted music box, and I'd fit
the key in the back of it, and twist—
and out would come the farmer and the wife,
child and nurse, dog and cat, the rat,
the wedge of porcelain cheese—
and that tinkling melody. On stifling
summer nights like this, I'd wind it up
tight, and lay back, and drift. . . .
          Hi ho the hairy hole,
            the shadow in the well.
Sorry. But honestly, how does it go?
The cheese stands alone, I think.
Surely you remember that much.

Do I disgust you?

He looks up from the table. Through the mist in his eyes he
stares at the pale circle shining in the black square of window.
The moon's standing over the town, he thinks. And not until
he douses the lamp does he see it was only his face. There is
no moon tonight. Outside, in the dark grass, the obsessive cricket
noise continues.

58

Something's rushing
through the low
green leaves. I think
fox (though foxes
don't thrive here) and rise
up onto one elbow on my
beachtowel raft,
peering at
the lilac hedge
that shimmers darkly—
as if some jaw were dragging
ragged wings over the cool
shadowed ground. Wind
noses up my back,
pawing my feathery
hair. *Just wind,*
I think, and lie down
trembling. Overhead, clouds
white, shifting, blown
to tatters on the same blue
Renaissance artists used
to make their foregrounded
humans loom. Yet
I don't believe we
loom like that. I know
what thrives in this place,
though not its name. I
know what thrives
in the blue, and it isn't
wind. I know we think
and think like drifting
on a raft . . . or
being blown to tatters
by our own breath. But how
overwhelming that smell
of lilac is! Listen:
I will be quiet
enough to let you listen.
Something is rushing
through the low
green leaves.

THE TREMBLING

Great are those hours when the trembling
stills in the hand, and the hand moves with easy
swiftness over the page, or with easy slowness
over the radiant body of a woman.

The rest of the time, it's better
not to lift a full cup of coffee
above important papers. Better not
to shave with a bright straight razor,
or stand on a ladder picking high apples.

It's better to work hard on solid ground—
digging, planting, weeding, sleeping.
Then the trembling enters the earth
like water, and the worms wiggle out
to escape the odd and uneasy vibration.

When I think how our trembling
will be squeezed out of us,
and what short work the worms
will make of our fine stillness,
I feel thankful.

Thankful for trembling, and for hours
of great calm when a ripeness comes unlike death,
and leaves us basking in the easeful radiance
of human bodies and human words.

CROSSING THE RIVER

for Susannah

The sky, after last night's wind, is bright
as the eyes of a child who's learned a new song,
and she comes to her father crying, "Listen!"

So he listens. He attends. But it's hard:
to hear what she hears, he must learn to love.

I noticed a woman on the bus one day. A red
birth-shadow flared across her left cheek.
She saw me staring; we each looked down;
the aisle became an impassable river.
If we'd talked? Oh, I'd never have risked
telling her what had first crossed my mind:
"I'll bet it tastes like strawberries."

Strawberries offer their seeds
frankly, not folded away in the core.
My eight-year-old likes them with cream,
a dust of sugar. They taste so good
that she can't keep from singing,
though her cheek's plump with fruit—
which I ought to remind her isn't polite.

But I listen instead. I attend. I am
learning how to hear the beauty she hears
as she sings with her sweet mouth full.

AS THE LATE SEPTEMBER DUSK COMES DOWN

for Brian

In the grassy slush of the fall's
first snow, my son, age three,
is dancing. He's dancing
this boot-heavy jig for joy—
or simply to drive out the ache
of an idle day indoors. He stamps
oblongs in the lumpy whiteness,
now and again gives a shout
made of steam. Then he halts
by the sagging apple tree
and stands a while, head back,
gazing through the ruined fruit,
into the failing light. Sure,
I should call him in. But I want
to savor that glad, forgiving look
that glows on his upturned face.

CAPE KIDNAPPERS, NEW ZEALAND
(After a photograph by Linda Pohle)

for Skip

The child's red hat floats
just above the reeds.
The sea she walks beside reaches
toward her, curling whitely,
slipping back. . . .

Each year a few more inches
of ash-gray volcanic soil crumble
off the cliffs, into the claws
of the waves. For a thousand years
the arbutus grove has been retreating
into the windy valley.

Far up that valley
the child's house stands—white,
slate-blue, grayish brown . . . door
the same ember color as her hat.
It all seems to float
just above the dark trees.

A thousand years. . . .

When we think of it, we know
that hats and doors are
sparks brief as scarlet glimpsed
under the blackbird's wing
in flight. . . .
One day, the sea swallows
all . . . and always
"too soon."

But the road home (the child's
feet know this) is long—
almost endless. . . .
And so she walks lightly,
at ease and patient, bearing
her small flame onward
into the ancient shadows
of the hills.

III
OPEN PLEASURES

CITY LIMITS

You're like wildwood at the edge of a city.
And I'm the city: steam, sirens, a jumble
of lit and unlit windows in the night.

You're the land as it must have been
and will be—before me, after me.
It's your natural openness
I want to enfold me. But then
you'd become city; or you'd hide
away your wildness to save it.

So I stay within limits—city limits,
heart limits. Although, under everything,
I have felt unlimited earth. Unlimited you.

CATACOMBS

And what will a man do
with his impossible love?
Love at cross-purposes
to other loves—what,

risk bringing it to light?
Think of Fellini's *Roma*,
when the tunnel diggers
stab through a stone wall

into some ancient catacomb.
The early Christians hid
and suffered there, in
despair and hope painted

faces—beautiful, haunting—
which the camera tenderly
lingers over; lingers even
as they blister and dissolve,

bathed by fresh air that burns
like the acid of time itself.
In the dark theatre, a man
wept to see it. And only now,

holding her face in mind,
in hiding, do I understand
why he wept—that man I was,
am still—against my will.

MEMORY (I)

The car hauled aside
to the shoulder by
sudden lust, our
hungry mouth-to-mouth
beneath a voluptuous
August moon. How
the whiskey's lullabye
lulled you, robbed
me of your sweet
resuscitation. Yet—
what you couldn't know—
there was the sleepy
warmth of your head
in my lap, the spill
of spun-gold hair
through my fingers
as I brushed it back,
the better to study
your face: more lovely
in our privacy than ever
I'd seen it. I wanted
never to move from there,
but did. Drove you home
to your obligations,
myself to mine. And now,
returned to the small
joys of dailiness, I
don't know what to wish
for us, unless that moon
and moment back again.
I bet that makes you
smile. "A lapse is all,"
I can almost hear you say,
"between friends. Okay?"
Sure. And yet, I need
to admit that I'm still
drunk on it, and like it.
Don't want to sober up
any time soon.

ADRIFT

I'm bearing your fine scent on my skin
like a soap bubble wearing a rainbow.
Don't know where the wind is taking me.
Can't tell how long or how far I'll drift.
Enough to float in this floating world,
wrapped in your fragrance, its colors
making my head and heart swim together.

COLD FRONT

At daybreak the east lay cloud-banked,
blue as veins in a wrist. A glittery mist
appeared and vanished on the windshield
as the wipers slapped, and my thoughts
came and went—each a small, clear drop
with your face inside it. I wondered
if we'd pass each other driving to work,
if the cold front was coming or going.
The distance between us hit me then,
hard—bruised me somehow, so that now
when I think of you it hurts to breathe.
And outside the cold front has settled in,
scattered rain across the office window.
Everywhere I look, I seem to find you.

COTTONWOOD MOON

Moon strong in the cottonwood,
on the moving creek water—
pouring its fresh cream
over your unbound breasts,
the warm skin of your stomach.

*

While our tongues wrestle,
the cottonwood rustles.
Leaves tickle down
all around us.

Higher up, a cloud
takes the moon tenderly
into its mouth, and shines.

*

Your back to my chest,
ass to lap—how snug
we fit! Breathing easy
under the cottonwood moon.

* (*charms*)

Against the blindness
of denial, that luminous
and soothing gaze of yours.

And your fragrance on my skin
against the pain of parting.

And against the bitter
hours without you,
sweet memory: everything
you say and do. Everything.

And our cottonwood moon
against the darkness.

AIR: "SOTTO VOCE"

More than wine or whiskey, your
sea-green glances make me reel.
I lean on anything to steady me—
a word, a silence—listening to my
blood's jazz weaving among my bones,
an ivy-like fountain of gladness.
You smile and the music flourishes;
leave, and its leaves fall still.
I bless whatever's planted this joy
around and in me, in us. Oh, sweet
addiction! Your eyes and smile;
your name *sotto voce* in my heart.

DAWN RIVER DRIVE (I)

Trees along the river at dawn,
dressed in your colors: gold,
red-orange, stubborn green.

They step slowly out of mist,
slip back into mist as I pass.

Overhead, flocks of wild birds;
a distant world calls them up
into desire, into confusion.
I watch them, and my heart
beats louder than the engine.

You've risen into my mind again.

I see you walking naked in lamplight;
see you naked in moonlight, arching
on the blanket; see you among friends
in your loose-fitting black pants;
see you in a chair, in cutoff shorts,
one foot up on the cushion, making
a tender bulge where the ragged
cuff bites your blonde thigh.

Scenes, as well, I've only heard of:
fleeing that violent man one November
in Bismarck, North Dakota (I can see
the snow-glitter's beautiful explosion
from the slammed door); or slipping
into a hospital bed with your grandma,
in front of strangers, to hold her
as you did when you were six.

And so much more. So many memories,
so much hearsay and invention!

And my heart pounding louder
than the engine as I drive
by the tree-lined river,
the river of fire and mist,
the river of birds and longing,
the river of love, at dawn.

DOUBT

After spending just one day apart, I
suddenly doubt: what is my love to you?
You with your fine hair spun from a topaz
held up in the clear, late-autumn light,

and your jade eyes flecked with umber,
and your panther's waist, and your voice
warm as a dove sheltering under the eaves
in the rain, and your kisses like grapes.

What can I be to you, in my common body?
The best of me given over to paper, words,
a torrent of breath in place of . . . what?

In place of what years have milled out of me,
what I find now only in you: mercy, wonder:
this desire I don't know how to deserve.

GRACE

Along the hogback, crosscut
to admit the highway straight
down into the valley, I took
a walking tour of the old
sea floor. Educational plaques
led me backward to Pliocene,
Paleocene, Cretaceous—
epochs squeezed into warped
striations, red and white,
gray and black: black
for the billion creatures
who rained down in death
through the primeval waters.
Nothing in my mind could stand
against it: time, pouring its
hemlock through my veins
until everyone I love became
images on film, their faces
speeding past the steady light
of what I knew: every day
we spend not loving is waste,
black stains in the rock! Then
tears with their ancient salt
came burning into my eyes,
and your name—sweet Melody—
flowed like grace on my tongue.

IRIS

Blue with yellow splashed
at the center, petals
open like folds of a high cloud
just after sunset, you're
lifted, little iris,
by a lithe green stem,
cool and smooth
to the touch, and I
lay you across her pillow
because of your beauty,
her favorite, simple
blue and yellow flame,
a kind of blessing
on this place
where her golden hair
will flow through my hands
like sunlight, spilling
all over my arms
as I lift her, warm
and smooth to the touch,
my favorite.

When I touch you, you lift up
the lamp of your blonde sex
with its curling rays of light,
and a brightness brims in my body:
light enough for a highway at night
or the darker paths of longing.

Our times together are so brief!
And apart, I am uprooted. I wander
among memories, which come and go
like fireflies in a wood. That's why
I devour your moist kisses like bread
still warm from the oven in winter.

You see, night is strong in me,
and your radiance has defeated it
as food defeats hunger—for a time.
And so I come back to you, touch
by touch, wanting more kisses,
more bread, more time, more light.

A BON VOYAGE

On the cruise ship, intense Carribean sun
dreams on your buttermilk skin: thighs,
stomach, shoulders lightly freckled
under your flaxen hair. The deck chair,

as I imagine it, is pink-and-white striped.
There's a drink with a decorative straw
and a lime slice on the rim. Laughter
flashes from the swimming pool like fish;

it makes you smile, but you don't look up:
the sun on your face is enough just now,
and the *thresh, thresh* of the hull
cleaving the blue waves, and the slap

of water on water the warm breeze carries
to your ears. Perhaps the deep serenity
of the moment's mixed with a little
emptiness . . . a space in your heart

my absence makes. Yet I hope you never
feel that absence—or so I tell myself.
What the hell *do* I want you to feel?
Pleasure is all. Nothing but pleasure!

WISH LIST

Your laughter each day.

A glimpse each day of your
warm waist, your breasts,
a little lovemaking
if the moment is ripe.

And the luminous green
of your eyes each day,
and your glittering hair.

Each day your fragrance
on my skin as I work,
and your mouth
on my mouth
at each day's end,
and your hand in my hand.

Your sanity in my craziness
like sweet cream in espresso.

My sanity in your craziness
like a mariner's compass.

Each day the sea-like
movements of love,
and its hush like sunlight
standing in the mist
among redwoods.

Each day your beauty
until all days are over,
all waking, all sleeping.

Your beauty each day.

MEMORY (II)

A clear light dreams on your gentle face,
bathes me as I watch you sleep, moves
through my mind like a balmy wind.
I remember drifting in a wooden boat
on some high-country lake: summer light
glinting off the water, and me lying back,
sun-washed, rocked by the sky's easy breath.
I must have been twelve, or even older,
allowed to row out alone and fish,
and I must have gotten sleepy or bored—
but all I remember is the calm: wind,
sun, the quiet talk of the waters.
After years of denial, years of rage,
it has found me again. The clear light
dreams on your gentle face . . . and I'm
drifting, drifting: watching you sleep.

SIREN

When the traffic thins, we
speed up. The sun's gone down,

and I'm following her. (We made
long love, got lit; I'm making

sure that she makes it home
alive.) My headlamp beams sweep

her car, glare in the rearview.
And suddenly I notice she's

drawing her fingers very gently
up through her love-tangled hair.

Indian Summer heat, I think; then
see she lifts her blonde locks

every time the traffic thins,
and we speed up. Don't know why,

and it makes me crazy—makes me
want to howl like a police car,

pull her over, kiss the moist
freckles on the back of her neck.

DAWN RIVER DRIVE (II)

Sun half up, a shimmer
in the winter mist,
like your heart
when you can't
catch your breath,
thinking of those moist
legs about your waist,
her mouth hot
against the artery
under your jaw—
that fire; and later,
the parting, driving home
in darkness and in tears,
as if the sun weren't ever
going to rise—but then
here it is, rising.
And soon, at your desk,
the phone will ring;
and tomorrow you'll lunch,
share drinks after work,
fresh kisses, fresh
lies for the ones
you need to deceive:
"It's temporary." Oh yes,
you believe it—because
now the sun's up,
and the next breath
pours into your chest
like time itself:
you can feel it
stinging as it heals
your torn heart again.

GOOD

I might have gone on with my heart in a pouch,
as a little boy hoards his favorite marble.
I might have gotten used to dining on crumbs,
living on the faintest taste: many have done it.

I might have learned to see in the dark, if dimly.
I might have learned to disremember the dreams
of tornados, and blasted tree limbs, and floods.
I might have learned to keep smiling for no reason.

I might have denied myself your kiss, your caress.
I might have sneered, "What's happiness worth?"
I might have let my duties define my desires.
I might have hurt no one. I might have been good.

Nearly two decades back, we stood
in the same cavernous hall and heard
the same music. A few months later

I would marry the woman I've left now,
and you'd go on into seventh grade.
Absurd to wish I'd have met you then—

we were different people, and life
doles out our chances at love
in its own good time. But still

I ache when I think of you there,
and me there, and the music we heard,
and the music we could not hear.

Embracing my guitar, perennial
amateur, I lift a heartfelt
sound from the strings,
now distorted, now almost
lovely, my small talent
coming and going like
a lighthouse beam
on the coast of night.
My struggle is to remain
faithful to the promise
of the music, which exists
not in the strung steel,
nor in the varnished body,
nor in my hands, but on
the margin between
the mind and the heart,
land and sea: a surf
that flows and glitters
like your hair in moonlight.
You see, you're the music
inside my almost-music,
the shining melody moving
among the progressions,
the difficult syncopations,
the bridges, the grace notes.
Which is why I turn to you
with my imperfectible skills,
my slow-learner's habits:
irony, doggedness, amazement;
my deep delight in making
good music, good love.

SUNBATHER

July's lavish heat has moistened
the tawny skin of your chest, almost
as lightly as this looking I can't
seem to check—aroused as I am
by your rosy composure. You lean
back a bit in your lawn chair, eyes
shut behind silver sunglass lenses.
Leaf-shade inches nearer at your feet,
but for now you're drenched in light.
And I find myself wanting to halt
the earth-wheel, keep the sun high,
not let any darkness touch you—
not even my own shadow. . . .

I remember a room full of weak fall light.
Your blood's sick, they said; don't cut yourself
(you'll keep bleeding), and don't go barefoot
down the hall, or you'll bruise your soles.
There were purple blotches on my shoulders
where I'd slept hard against the bed's sidebars,
which they lowered only to bathe me. Baths
are what I remember best. Yes: water
warm in its sponge, then cool on my skin;
the palely freckled hands of the Irish nurse,
her voice like a tree full of summer wind:
"Lift up your hip, please. Relax, just relax,
don't pull away. How's that feel now?" It felt
soothing, safe, being so gently cared for—
the way you always make me feel: bathed
in beauty, lifted and healed, my heart
repeating the one good thing that illness
taught me: *Relax, just relax. Don't pull away.*

OPEN PETALS

Wondering if right now you're
drinking from the cup I gave you,
china-white with blue irises—
petals loosely open, the leaves
sharp and delicate and green.

Your gift to me, a pottery mug,
is full and close at hand: sides
tall, ribbed when the spinning
clay was wet, then glazed brown
and painted over with irises.

Lifting it, drinking, I wonder
if we sip at the same moment,
touching the same open petals.
Thinking of it steals my breath—
how your lips must feel on the rim.

AFTER ALL THESE YEARS

When I fantasize your kisses it
rattles me, like downing four
mugs of coffee in advance
of noon, making me tremble
unnervingly through the whole
lunch hour. But your real kisses,
when they come to me, calm me
like half a valium chased
with beer, so that my convict
heart stops banging its cup
on the bars—because the iron
door has suddenly shuddered open,
and the guard's waving me out,
waving me out with a smile
after all these years.

My whiskey's iced, your vodka's
iced and vermouthed (its two
stuffed olives nailed together
with a tiny plastic sword),
when your hair suddenly
takes the rich tavern-light:
I *see* you, and my heart expands,
and lust plumps in my pocket.

But I need to behave myself.

I need to remember the others,
patrons, waitresses, bartenders,
all the eyes that would widen
if I slid to my knees and lifted
your skirt and kissed the skin
all up and down your thighs.
I have to behave myself,
and not unbutton your blouse
with easy, breeze-like motions,
and not unhook your bra-strap
like a magician's assistant,
and not drink in the fragrance
of your breasts and bite them
tenderly—just so, just so.

My God, I've got to behave!

I've got to manage my whiskey
and choke on propriety's collar
and meekly swallow its times—
right times, wrong times—
when all I want is love time.

All I want is you.

BLESSINGS

Open kiss, open smile. The open
pleasure of gliding in and out
of your body in the swimming pool,
in the company of unknowing strangers.

*

Drawing on your summer-hot skin
with an acorn-sized nugget of ice.
Throat to nipple, rib to navel,
meltwater trickling from the tips
of my fingers, into your rosy folds.

*

And the ordinary joy in plain
touch: my hand on your bare hip,
the crook of my arm tenderly
cradling your head as you sleep.
Listening to the curtain lift
and lift: the afternoon breeze
cat-footing over our bodies
in the ordinary bedroom.

*

I shall not have time enough
ever in this life to finish
thanking you—which
is yet another blessing.

AT THE MIRROR

Watching you primp before getting dressed:
striped panties like sunlight through blinds,
tender curve of stomach kissing the sink's edge;
a long-toothed comb drawn through crimped locks,
then the hair dried from dark blonde to gold,
the dryer whining, blowing hard and hot;
then the eyes, the clear eyes, the lashes;
lotions, powders, sprays, to each a purpose;
and you purposeful, intent as you finish—
twist and tuck, pat and look—looking
deep into the mirror that does not love you,
as if it might reveal what only I can show you:
I who stand waiting for you to turn and see.

Was it truly love, do you think?
Oh, it was love. *Did it heal you,*
this love? I still knew sickness,

suffered rage and fear; but yes,
love healed me. *But your body?*
Love was good to my body

as long as my body was good.
And your soul? Always broken;
most days I'd feel it grating

like pottery shards in a sack
I had to carry. *Yet you claim*
you were healed. There was

a shattered something in me,
not body or soul; I could never
look quick enough—caught

only glimpses: some presence
made of splinters, it seemed;
then love, and where splinters

drifted like blown smoke, a tall
tree rose. I could shut my eyes
and feel its roots stretching,

feel the needles sifting wind.
And then you died? And then
I died. *Why, if it was love?* Look:

this tree we two are sitting under,
from which I crept like a shadow
toward sunset: this is death—

but *my* death. Love healed it,
helped it grow; now it shelters
even you—my double, my doubt.

ABOUT THE AUTHOR

Joseph Hutchison is the author of one previous full-length collection of poems, *The Undersides of Leaves*, and five chapbooks, including *Sweet Nothing Noise* and *Shadow-Light*. The latter was chosen by poet Richard Shelton to be the 1982 Colorado Governor's Award volume. Hutchison's poems have appeared in such publications as *American Poetry Review*, *The Hudson Review*, *Mississippi Review*, *The Nation*, *Ohio Review*, *Poetry (Chicago)*, and in several anthologies. Most recently, he co-edited the anthology *A Song for Occupations: Poems About the American Way of Work* (Wayland Press, 1991). He resides in Denver and makes his living as a writer.